Watermelon Seeds

David Thomasson

iUniverse, Inc.
Bloomington

Watermelon Seeds

iUniverse books may be ordered through booksellers or by contacting:

iUniverse
1663 Liberty Drive
Bloomington, IN 47403
www.iuniverse.com
1-800-Authors (1-800-288-4677)

Because of the dynamic nature of the Internet, any web addresses or links contained in this book may have changed since publication and may no longer be valid. The views expressed in this work are solely those of the author and do not necessarily reflect the views of the publisher, and the publisher hereby disclaims any responsibility for them.

Any people depicted in stock imagery provided by Thinkstock are models, and such images are being used for illustrative purposes only.

Certain stock imagery © Thinkstock.

ISBN: 978-1-4502-9549-9 (sc)
ISBN: 978-1-4502-9550-5 (ebook)

Printed in the United States of America

iUniverse rev. date: 03/24/2011

Should eyes never fall upon these pages
and ears never hear these words.
Still I feel greatly relieved having expressed
my inner thoughts.

David L. Thomasson

Dedication

These simple writings are dedicated to Celine, my wife, who is the trinity of my love:

- The charming and beautiful lady of my days,
- The sensual woman of my nights, and,
- The innocent child of my dreams.

Hopefully, she will find here the deep and adoring love reserved exclusively for her and only her. And if there is beauty here, it is only my feeble attempt to describe the inner feelings that spring to my mind whenever she is near. As always, pitiful and unashamed of my love…David

CONTENTS

POEMS

OTHER WRITINGS

POEMS

Watermelon Seeds

You remind me of watermelon seeds
So hard to put a finger on
Shooting off to escape the slightest pressure
And yet, once firmly secured
You are the source of great enjoyment
And even pleasure

The Perfect End to the Perfect Day
(Her Poem)

How I'd love one day
to see your body
drenched with sweat
glistening in the scorching sun
your face, a handsome face
rugged and burned
after hours of work, work, work
your hands
strong and beautiful
but calloused
from forgetting your gloves
and as you near, your smile
telling me what's in your mind
letting me know
you are glad to be home
and that all of you
is still loving all of me.

The Perfect End to the Perfect Day
(His Poem)

How I'd love one day
to return to the house
tired from working in the field
burned from the heat of the sun
blistered from forgetting my gloves
to see you watching
a wave of your hand
a toss of your head
your eyes bright and lonely
in a special way
your jeans and cotton shirt
so simple, and yet, so provocative
your laugh like music on the wind
lifting my spirit
telling of the love still in your heart
letting me know
you're glad to have me home
and that all of you
is still loving all of me.

Homecoming

It was your step
upon the threshold
my heart stopped
for a moment
anticipating
until the door filled
with your smile
your eyes so swift
to find my face
your laugh
which followed
my heart

A Temporary Thing

Yellow roses
as all worldly things
eventually deteriorate
the petals fall
to remind of lonely tears
from unrequited love
which run down pains of being
to form great pools
and stand in mute testimony
to love
a temporary thing

Love Will Endure
(Ode to the Bride)

Wait
though time stands stagnant
a pool in August
time matters not
love will endure.

Love is the sun
undiminished by eternity
yet, be impatient
as lovers are prone to do
pace the floor.

Although
it will not make you love more
or less
and, when it is time
come softly.

Shoes in hand, hair about your face
to let my clumsy fingers
remove your gown of lace
and kiss your lovely body
in every secret place.

Wounded Angel's Lament

The cries of pain all about
make me worrisome
who will make it through the night
only hope I'm one
but Father dear in heaven
if I must come to Thee
could you forgive my many sins
and bring my mom to me?

She worried so when I left
that I would catch a cold
and Lord, her hair was turning gray
my mom was getting old
you know, I'd be on my knees
if only that I could
but one is gone completely
the other feels like wood.

It's true a lot of sin can happen
in seventeen years
so if I don't deserve a favor
perhaps my mama does
she was always such a good woman
taking care of dad and me
she worked her fingers to the bone
and never said a word
once dad said, she screamed in pain
the morning of my birth.

And you know, she'd want to see me
before I leave this earth
thank you Lord, she's at my side
her tears, they wash my face
her hand is on my fevered brow
it's time I left this place
goodbye mama, I love you so
don't give my dog away.

Signed "A Marine"

The Circus

My dad, mom, sister and me
went to the circus its sights to see

Its music led us out of town
people were parked all around

We walked past colored tents so gay
bordering the sides of the midway

Animals were in cages kept
one was a tiger who quietly slept

Sister pulled the tiger's ear
and when it roared, jumped in fear

Next, we came to a funny clown
who rode a tricycle round and round

There were balloons and cotton candy
throwers of knives so handy

People on swings high above
some diving down into a tub

We laughed the whole night through
and finally, could find nothing more to do

But the important thing had been done
passing the time in family fun.

I Saw You in a Golden Globe

And the sun reflected
from the golden globe
as I reached down
and cupped it into my hand
it sparkled and turned warm
to the touch.

Opening my palm slightly
I gazed at this orb
it cleared and inside
was a green valley
you were there
alone.

Solitary by choice
afraid to trust in trust
trusting only in your fear
of being hurt
arms reached for you
but with a sweep of your hand
you pushed them away.

They were adornments
to entertain, to be taken
or discarded at will
and as I watched
the leaves began to turn
and you cried out
"the price of strength
is the cost of living alone."

The Marlin Inside of Me

Eyes as black as printer's ink,
Round and dead as the drain in a sink,
Silver sides shimmer like mink,
He'll never give up, he's a brut I think.

Adam, he pulls with all his might,
Kyle, he comes to join the fight,
Steam from the reel in a cloud rose,
Sweat from their bodies as if from a hose.

Throw water over them or they'll die of the heat,
Some on their heads, the rest on their feet,
Sixty minutes the battle raged,
A more fitting contest could never be staged.

The reel sang in a rising whine,
The boat in reverse will it be in time,
Finally, he jumps ten feet in the air,
A sword tipped missile, a ton I swear.

Down to the bottom, he sank like a tomb,
He bent the hook straight as a harpoon,
My friend, Hector, my two sons, and me,
Battled a creature from the deep blue sea.

There's no film to tell of it all,
No stuffed fish on my office wall,
Just the marlin inside of me,
And the happy feeling he's still free.

Snails. . .

Aren't smart
Aren't fast
Aren't pretty

Don't have personality
Don't have ambition
Don't have enthusiasm

Can't smile
Can't laugh
Can't cry

But they get by
How about you?

Without Strings

My kite soars above
tugging to be free
but I only pull the string
teasing it to fly higher
my rebellious kite doesn't know
of my longing to fly
without strings.

Cinco de Mayo

Kneeling quietly,
the Mexicans watched,
through eagle eyes,
a river of steel approach,
the sun flashed,
from the hungry blades,
of bayonets,
dust a shroud,
drifted over those soon to die,
and yet, they did not shirk,
or flee,
before the French army.

And the French shouted,
Sons of Mexico, where are your shoes?
Sons of Mexico,
where are your rifles?
Sons of Mexico,
where are your cannons?
Sons of Mexico,
did you kiss your mothers goodbye?

But there was no panic here,
deep in each heart,
was the flame,
the burning flame,
of freedom, nationalism, patriotism,
courage picked them up as one,
and with a great cry,
they fell upon the French
the finest army in the world paused,
then staggered,
and the French wondered,
what manner of men are these?
to hurl themselves,
without weapons,
into the jaws of death?

And that day, the 5ᵗʰ of May 1862,
the battlefield was covered,
with fine uniforms,
with new boots,
with weapons and cannons,
and the dead and dying French,
and that day,
the first sons of Mexico,
were immortalized,
covered with glory
with honor and victory,
and people of the world,
impoverished people,
people without weapons or uniforms,
took courage.

Is the 5ᵗʰ of May important to Mexicans?
Yes, of course,
Is it more?
Yes, much more,
because it is a salute to every heart,
where the fire of liberty,
nationalism, and patriotism burns,
it is hope to the oppressed,
My God, I would be proud to be a Mexican,
on the 5ᵗʰ of May,
or any other day.

We Got Our Limit

Birds on wing
against the sky
clouds adrift
and you and I

Dog on point
granite friend
a rock unmoving
until the end

And as we troop
back to the truck
it matters not
if we had luck

Breaking Up

A sand castle collapsed
before my eyes
a dream of love
washed away by the tide
taking promises
leaving empty shells
but in returning
to where it began
it left its mark
upon the sand.

Don't Stop

Yes, it is I
the imbecile
of your enigma
traveling
we meet
in the night
in flight
two birds
of a feather
we flock
and flock
until we can
flock no more
evermore
into the sun
forever and ever

Insignificance

A star fell last night
its lamp snuffed no more to light
and as I watched from my bed
my heart filled with senseless dread
of what we had done and all we had said
and as my thoughts turned to you
and the barriers between we two
and also considered the sky above
nature, life, and even love
my mind was caught in this interval of time
where nature's power was all sublime
and before it passed I knew for sure
my feelings for you would endure
but knowing also it mattered little at all
in relation to why a star should fall.

Who Was That Masked Man?

On the back roads
on the trails
in smoky places
they travel
for an interval in time
ships in the night
floating on rivers of lies
into lakes of deceit
passing, pausing, stopping
but to what purpose?

A trip of uncertain destiny
not knowing what they seek
sufficing in the hunt, the capture and release
lovers bound together
in the perversion of their normality
until they ask all:
are you from the straight world?
or the underworld?
from the world we appear to live in?
or from the world we live in?

Often, the country rag picker
the washer woman
they sort through their roles
those falling in the wrong stack
must be separated
co-mingling is unwise
until they die
and their relatives ask
"Who were all those strangers
at the funeral?"

Why I'd Like to Be a Cypress Tree

Cypress trees
In silent majesty stand
Feet in water
Heaven in hand
Limbs outstretched
Umbrella of life
Quiet observer
Of natural strife

The Devil's Workshop

They cross my mind
subconscious to conscious
fleetingly
never pausing
passing between rational realities
dreams, desires
faces twisted, ugly
or pure and clean
bodies cavorting, acrobatic
different partners
sometimes more than one
some beautiful
some young
occasionally animals
from what cause?
to what end?

One With the Universe

The sun's fingers
probe the dark
it is dawn
still quiet
not yet violated
the day like a new bride
waits in anticipation
of the coming rush
a gentle breeze touches my face
to remind of you
now gone
from our love-warmed bed
your scent a butterfly
drifts through the air
to bring pleasant thoughts
and memories
sufficient to sustain
until we return again
to become one with the universe.

Stop
(To the President)

Hang a moon
as one must
late in the month
before the trees
can see it wane
and as eyes turn to stars
and mouths to bars
and echoing steps
of the donkey's hooves
click, clack
on the cobblestones
to say
move over
there's room for
another ass at the top
Stop!

Would You?

The baby coughed all week before she died
and we had no money for medicine
so take me to the old buildings
where the wharf rats run pitter, patter
and toss me to the slime-covered streets
smash me in the broken dreams of the poor
and break my bones to bits
let me die among the shattered hopes
the frustration, the slow death of poverty
turn my skin black, so the despair of discrimination
can course through my mind
let my children wallow in the cesspool of ignorance
chain them to this culture of misery
let the roaches run in my mouth where I lay
then tell me to wait.

The Cycle

Words scratched on the walls,
trash and litter in the halls,
plaster piled up where it falls,
Identify.

Laughter forgotten in the past,
happy moments gone so fast,
tears hanging on 'til last,
Exemplify.

Children coughing in the night,
families screaming as they fight,
broken wine bottles that didn't make it right,
Amplify.

Cops with frowns that walk the beat,
the smell of sweat in the stifling heat,
thugs and hookers on the street,
Testify.

People standing in welfare lines,
panhandlers begging for dimes,
churches which preach of better times,
Rectify.

School dropouts abound,
unemployed standing around,
idle people always found,
Justify.

Fire plugs gushing on a summer day,
stickball games under the freeway,
mothers wishing they could run away,
Preoccupy.

Crooked teeth in need of braces,
deserted cars and junky places,
empty stomachs and angry faces,
Intensify.

Government designs which never work,
food stamps given to the grocery clerk,
duties we'd rather shirk,
Indemnify.

Agamemnon

On opposite hills they gathered
The one hovering like buzzards
The other with wings to the sky
One side shouted, "Give me death"
the other, "Give me life"

No compromise was possible
The stranger on horseback paused
Reined in as he passed between them
And the prince of darkness spoke
"Death is eternal, but life
like smoke in the wind is temporary
Which do you choose?"

And the stranger whispered
"Give me life"
And the stranger said aloud
"Give me life"
And he shouted, "Give me life
I stand for life"

Fire Inside

There is a fire
that burns inside
its heat at times
I cannot abide
but most of the time
its flame is small
no pain or heat
from it at all.

Ode to a Dead Roach

Oh! Dead roach laying there,
How did you come to such a sad end?
Was your passing silent?
Or did screams rent the air?
Did you meet the grim reaper alone?
Or with your grimy friends?
Just look at you, a sad state of repair,
Tumped over on your back,
Your wheels no longer turning,
Your headlights have lost their glow,
Your aerial crooked and bent,
A sad fate, even for someone so abhorred.
Were you gassed or simply crushed?
Were you killed in a Christian way?

The Hunt

Let me come along fellows
a mass of dark locks
so curly

I'll carry your rock bucket
large brown eyes, so innocent
and I won't scare the birds

Jumping from one nimble foot
to the other
so pleadingly

Please, you guys
a small impish face
so serious

I'll do just what you ask
a toe drug in the sand
so longingly

I'll put my cap on
and no one'll know I'm a girl
two little cheeks crossed by tears

A Lady in Waiting

Spring
light as a butterfly's kiss
touches the land
plants break through the snow
straining to reach the sun
animals stir impatiently
in their dens
birds sing of earth
a lady in waiting
for the eternal cycle
and yet
winter's chill hangs
like an undertaker's coat
soberly
in the background
to remind
birth
is always difficult.

Only the End

Like a captive river
its torrent bound
our lives pool
swirl
back up
waiting
the opportunity
to pour
to overflow
all
in the path
rushing toward destiny
it matters not
what is twisted
broken
swept away
only the end
is important

The Dungeon

You seem
the last rose
of summer
a Thanksgiving
bonus

But are you an illusion
to fade so quickly
leaving only the wounds
where the thorns pricked

If not, come to me
whirlwind of daggers
meet your gardener
be pruned of
your sticky ways

For I will have you
to fill my senses
but know in coming
you will never leave
the dungeon of my memory

Me Either

Life is difficult to understand
it slips away
slips away
until in desperation
by force
we must
live it
against our will
or won't
or maybe
everything I hate involves getting older

If God is perfect
why do people age?
Is it to make room
for other 12 year old children?
between child and adult
caught in a happiness of time
caring for neither but caring
awaking each day to a new joy
not doubting its source
not waiting for the falling hammer
just living the moment to its fullest

Maybe My Sample Was Too Small

How she loved dogs
she always had one
to kiss her face
and to sleep at her feet
when the weather was cold

But she hadn't even seen
this particular dog
it just ran out soundlessly and bit her
no barks, no growls
only the pain on her calf

And then the shots
in the stomach, of course
the most sensitive spot
they were much more painful
than the bite

Twenty-eight times to the doctor
the sweaty palms, the clammy body
the fear of pain, the smell of alcohol
and the needle, at least three inches long
and big as a match

Her stomach knotted
at the memory
and it was just a memory
from twenty years before
she had hated dogs ever since

Now she had no dogs
traitors that they were
bite the hand that loved her
or the leg or
whatever was available

She always called the grocery store
and had the groceries delivered
why she hadn't even
been out of the house
in all those twenty years

But she had proven the master
she was the strongest
she could give up something
dogs couldn't cause her pain
without suffering the consequences

Why she would probably
have loved one dearly
all this time, been a great companion
ran through the park, grown old together
had it not been for one mad dog

She looked down at the wrinkled skin on her hand
and in the mirror at the age in her eyes
and the gray in her hair, at the tattered dress
and thought: I won, I won, or did I?
Maybe my sample was too small

We Never Speak of It

Often when we're close
when our smiles mingle
becoming one happiness
when our lips touch
and our laughter
rises above worldly cares
butterflies on the wind
I feel you want to relate
your feelings.

Much can be read
from body language
but some things
should be said
not often
not until they become
tired worn terms
but in the confidence
such feelings are mutual.

Will you let me
crawl on my knees
longing to know
we have love
in common
I will
because
we never
speak of it.

Sail Dog

Once there was
a barking dog
Who bit at passing auto tires
And that's the key
"Once, there was."

The Nature of Thee
(Ode to Stubbornness)

Climbing the snow-covered alps
in February wasn't difficult

Swimming the mighty Amazon
during the rainy season was easy

Walking a tightrope over the Grand Canyon
with a tornado blowing was a piece of cake

Running nude through a field of thorny cactus
was a summer breeze

But telling you I love you and making you believe
and trust me, now that's really hard

And I'm not even sure it can be done
so just let me say I do

And then you believe whatever you want
you are going to anyway

Never Say Goodbye

The day you did not come I sat alone
With eye of tear and heart of stone
Memories then returned
As if to show a lover spurned

Darkness was here and I was alone
With thoughts and dreams
At last you came
My feelings still the same
My heart was light and gay
My soul cried out to a new day

And, alas, as at first you were gone
Leaving me with my heart of stone
And then I knew my fate was to cry
But wait and never, never say goodbye

Into My Mind

Into my mind I crawled
until the thoughts passed like bullets
in a western movie
zipping, bouncing off the wall, shouting
"Don't worry about what
you can't do anything about"

Nearby was a gauge on the wall
and the arrow on the gauge
shot into the red
and the dead man with a crooked leg said
"Don't ask me anything else
the pressure is too great"

And the weather vane turned into the wind
as the crowd held its breath
and the buzzards circled above
and a mouse stirred in its nest
as an owl in the wilderness cried
"There isn't anything else
no matter what the pressure
what is is and what isn't doesn't matter"

So let the pressure rise and
let the boiler blow
and the chips fall
where they may
and if an arm is lost
or an eye blown out
so be it and the devil
take the hind most

Pool of Tears

Once upon a sunset
as locust hummed
October death songs
from oak trees
which lurked near
thoughts began to form
thunderheads threatening peace
despair, a newly filled tomb
stood in testimony
to this day apart and distinct
forever lonely
to tell of dreams
discarded by choice
into a pool of tears
where widening circles spread
until violated and broken
they washed ashore
as if to ask
Why?

Why?

I grew from an infant
as a flower in the field
natural and beautiful
and sometimes circumstances
behoove me to return
to the protection of the womb
to the safety of childhood
to escape the insecurity of life
the doubt, but on these occasions
the question is always - why?

A question never adequately answered
as the reason is difficult to grasp
like smoke in the wind
or a bar of soap in warm water
so when the sun rises
on the world the next morning
and on my sleep-tossed bed
a face peers from the reflection of my mind
as thoughts bounce from the widening ripples
and the lips mouth - why?

Often the answer booms from the cliffs
to the valleys and back to the clouds
shouting
"to deceive, to be cruel
to hurt, to play games"
like echoes in the cave of the bats
whirlpools in the river
dust devils in the desert
now here, now there
now gone forever

But before it disappears
recognized as a likely cause
delayed childhood
but on occasion the answer is
"to love, to give compassion
to fulfill and complete"
like blossoms in the spring
birds on the wing
friends at Christmas
always there

Then I realize
the situation
is but a sham
a charade
another dream
for no one acts childish
for these reasons
and pinch myself awake
to the reality of the world
and only ask - why?

A Black Cloud Blew Over the Moon Last Night

A black cloud blew over the moon last night
And there were those it gave a fright
They even said, "it just ain't right!"
For the devil has covered our natural light

Others, weren't so sure the speakers were right
And didn't trace the cause to the devil's might
Nor did they consider it a worldly plight
The darkness to them was simply nature's delight

Love is the Purpose

Love is all there is
Without love
Life is meaningless
Without love
One unhappy day
Follows another
An endless stream of gloom
A hell to be endured
Between birth and death

Love has no limits
It can include
Love of another
Love of self
Love of parents
Love of nature
Love of country
Love of people and
Love of life

So why love?
Because love
Is the purpose of life

Beyond the River

As we stood above the river
swift and dangerous
wild and deep
the specter of death spread
pale images
on the reflective surface
calling to mind the frailty of life.

And we pondered
in the crossing
which of us might die
and I thought
if someone must
better it be me
than to live without you.

This thought was echoed
in your eyes
the same
and without a word
we walked
hand-in-hand
into the water.

Words of Love?

From time-to-time
your letters fall
from their drawers
tired and worried
from many readings.

They turn my thoughts
to romance, to love
to promises and pledges
invariable tears follow.

For no matter
what the words say
they only mean
Goodbye!

The Color of Love

What color is love?

Is it red
of passion
of desire
of anger and emotion?

Is it blue
of reason
of stability
of tranquility and peace?

Is it pink
of softness
of compassion
of dim lights and music?

Is it yellow
of cowardice
of deception
of lying and cheating?

No,
it's not the rainbow
but the pot of gold
for those who find it.

Thanks to You

Yesterday
I pulled a tooth with a pair of pliers
It was tough getting a grip
The pliers were large
My mouth small
But then just twist
From side-to-side
And snap, out it comes
Oh, sure it bled for a few hours
And hurt a few days
But now it's fine.

It would have been impossible
But I thought of you
The pain when you left
It was tough getting a grip
But then just plunge the knife in
Twist from side-to-side
Oh, sure I bled for a few months
And hurt for a few years
But now it's fine

Goodbye My Love

May the sun always shine for you
And the clouds fade away

May smiles fill your basket
With many a happy day

May you live in peace and harmony
All the days of your life

And find that love
Of a special kind

Never regretting
Who you've left behind

Hate Me

Hate me for what I am
But not for what you are

Hate me for what I do
But not for what you do

Hate me for my inadequacies
But not for your inadequacies

Hate me for using you
But not because you are using me

Hate me for my weakness
But not because you are weak

Last, let us love while we can
As hate will come soon enough

Parents in the Background

They are always there
Ready to speak

"We lived our lives for you
Think of us before you act
Honor our beliefs
Our lives, smoke in the wind
Will soon be gone
Would you make us realize our inadequacies?
Among all things we created you
Would you blemish our perfection?"

Such ties are hard to overcome
Almost impossible to break
No matter how selfish a person may be
They form a large part of
What we call our conscience
And prevent a complete adjustment
to changing morals

For the Individual

Polar bear rugs are so big and soft
so furry and warm
so nice to lay on before a fire
and yet, there is latent strength
power asleep, turned off, bound inside.

Trees are so tall and stately
so green and full of life
so nice to climb and swing in
and yet, there is latent strength
power asleep, turned off, bound inside.

Rings are golden and round
they encircle and bind
without beginning and without end
and yet, there is latent strength,
power asleep, turned off, bound inside.

Such is the nature
of polar bear rugs
trees, rings
they bind the
power of living things.

Looking in the Mirror

Weddings are beautiful
so pure, so white
so refreshing and cleaning
they renew, begin, initiate
a cycle never ending
again and again

Over and over, lips in unison move
steps follow steps, one after the other
two by two like paired geese
forever, through life
as it was in the beginning
it is now and will ever be

The hand of destiny reaching into the masses
selecting from a sea of faces two people
once marked they begin the expected dance
old things cast aside
bright lights, strange mates,
and all unrestricted living discarded

Sobriety and monogamy are cherished
like forgotten friends
new beings are adorned with the strangers they should be
the self is suppressed, the monster chained
looking in the mirror they see the composite
and not the individual

Communication – Don't Expect It of Me

If I could, I would tell you
What was in my heart today
I would rip it from my chest
To reveal its hidden secrets

It wouldn't be a pretty sight
Criss-crossed with scars
Pains from the past
Once searing, now healed

The origin forgotten
Blocked from the mind
To preserve sanity
But one would be fresh

Its source not forgotten
Still lingering in my thoughts
If I could tell you
What was in my heart today

Can't Say

Can't say I love you
But I like you
Like the *sky* likes clouds
Like birds like eggs
Like beavers like trees
And, like turtles like ponds
'Cause can't say I love you

Because

For all the times I've made you mad
For all the fun we've ever had
For the many mean things that I do
But most of all because I love you

Our Love

Our love, a star
Lights up the heavens
of my nights
and never pales
before the morning light

In Training to Become God

Butter-salt colored flowers
Spread a yellow mantel
Over meadows of green
Birds build nests
Ants scurry to and fro
Creatures great and small
All work to fulfill their destiny
I watch

Alone

Come, let's laugh
While we may
And sip summer wine
Until the neon lights fade
And the silence shrouds
The hollow feeling left
To speak of the lonely
And we reach for each other
In fear

Poems

Poems, cats on the roof
Can't be caught
They spring, not from the pen
But to the ground
Why can't they run between the lines?
Perhaps, if they did
We'd have too many

A Voice in the Wilderness

I heard a bird the other night
In the black a voice of fright
Singing away with all its might
Wishing the dark would turn to light

We could learn from this small bird
Silent voices are never heard
But when we sing or shout
The air is cleared, we get it out

So let me urge my fellow man
Peace of mind is near at hand
Take your burdens to God above
He'll share them all with boundless love

Pride Is

Pride is the lion, love is the lamb
and they cannot lay together
for the lion will devour the lamb
so, they who would love
must first slay the lion
unsheathe your knife
stand with me
united our strength will multiply
and no beast can stand before us

And when it is done, come to me
you warrior woman
you slayer of lions
and still the raging beast in me
the beast that hungers
for your sweet flesh
for as gentle
as my love for you is
it is also brutal

So, cut me that I will know your love
is not taken without pain
as well as pleasure
for pain and pleasure
are petals of the same flower
and as you come
feel my teeth sink into your shoulder
and know the force of my passion
press yourself to me with strength

So we may try physically
what already is mentally
and when you are finished with me
cast me aside to see if the beast pride is really dead
and if I laugh and if we see the humor of it all
then, let's do it again and again
for if we grow tired of each other
let us do it in the love of each other
and go our separate ways

Hello Yesterday

The crowd knelt and silently chanted
this we pray that the stillness of last night
be called back to determine if it was
justified in passing, in giving way
to the light, the light that ended the night
was it right, or should it have stayed
to cloak, to quiet
and many stood to witness, crying out
this day has brought no joy
we condemn it for anger and frustration
we convict it of sadness.

It should be executed for misery
the jury danced out, the jury danced in
leg-to-leg, back-to-chest
hunched over like Groucho Marx
flicking their cigars, curling their mustaches
and said, the defendant is guilty of all charges
and must forfeit all rights
must give up the light and is sentenced
as lips moved in unison to return to last night
goodbye today, hello yesterday
this we pray, amen.

Flowers

Flowers remind me of you
Because they are
Reserved and beautiful
Silent and stately
Moving in natural ways
Lovely with drops of water on their limbs
Smelling of their own particular odor
Flowers are also rooted in the ground
Stubborn and resistant to winds of change
Always taking love and never returning it
Yes, flowers remind me of you

Did You Call?

Two hats, a cat, and some children dear
set the stage for a tale of cheer
was upon a day so very clear
long ago, yet seemingly near
when the wind blew up
a frightful storm
with sufficient force
to do property harm

Children were playing in an open field
straw hats blew off against their will
fearing the wrath of their parents dear
they chased the hats far and near
but the hats were always beyond their reach
so they went to a cat, who they did beseech
to aid them in their failing quest
saying, "please aid us cat we do request"

With tail in the air and nose to the ground
the cat jumped to the job with a mighty bound
quick as a wink the hats were retrieved
and the children were overjoyed at being reprieved
so the cat was granted his fairest wish
to drink some milk and eat a fish
so, if your hat is beyond your reach
ask for help or even beseech

It Would Have to Do

Alone again
just the radio
for company
with a song
about love
reminding of the
forever lonely feeling
of being without you
out-of-body travel
would be nice
to be able to reach
in the spirit
for you

I'm All Right, You're...?

It came drifting on the wind
like a bird song or a falling leaf
or perhaps, a thistle seed
making its difficult journey
to my understanding
it was a feeling
physical, yes
mental, yes
indefinable but distinct
as in losing at anything
as in sinking, as when the moon is full
as when you have a cold
a rotten, beaten down depression
shouting in rage, breaking a chair in anger
throwing a bottle through the glass
did little good.

Eventually, I realized why
it was like a gas leak
seeping from an unknown source
breaking down natural optimism
destroying normal elevation
being of simple mind I could only ask why?
Why? Echoed through the chambers of my mind
beat on the door of my subconscious
behind which the answer lurked
and, much like a dirt dauber in the wind
after having been blown from place-to-place
with no further adieu, arrived at its resting place
and as the dust fell from the blood red sun
and the cataracts from my eyes
what was hidden suddenly became clear
I'm all right but how are you, my dear?

They All Did

The judge said the choice is yours
life in prison or death
smash my palm on the table
leap to my feet, voice loud and clear
give me death, yes death
bring the grim reaper
kill me, kill me
better death
than life without my love

now on death row
bars cold on my cheek
workers below
ants of death
building the gallows
life is finite
and the end is near
pace the cell
like a caged animal

pull a wire from the bed
pick the lock across the wall
to your door reaching for your hand
shot down
who fired?
the Police?
society?
my family?
your family?

Will No One Share the Burden?

Time of endless dread
where lips are stone and
faces adorned with muted ears peer
in silent testimony
to the self-castration of life
as we scream in widening echoes
to pierce the vale of frustration
but, to no avail

Our great granite God
this benevolent being
turns the other cheek
like a broken weather vane
always facing the wind
the despair
the inhumanity
will no one share the burden?

Parents

Gosh, it's hard when your parents get old
You realize what a rotten child you were
So, Mom and Dad
I apologize for wanting the white meat
and not the neck

When God Died

A raven with one eye
perched on a crooked limb
of a twisted tree and speaking
in a broken voice, said
"Do thee have need of me?"
A newborn deer tilted an ear
to hear the raven's speech so clear
and repeated the words with cheer
"Do thee have need of me?"
And it echoed throughout the land
far away and near to hand
and soon became an animal pray
and even spread to the human fair
and all could plainly see
there was no need of he for me

Death Chant
(Ode to Marriage)

When but a child spoke as an adult
thought as a child of duty, of escape
of life and love, paid like a criminal
for a faulty decision made without experience
no judge could reduce the self-imposed sentence
of loss of normal childhood
of loss of the pleasure of adulthood
torn by the struggle between the child and adult
with no chance for parole
to serve until death do us part.

Fist beat on the familiar table
forehead pressed on its cool surface
tears cross my face, soul cries for release
reach out hoping to be purged of guilt
of the hurt, the hate, the love
these hopeless sentiments beating like rain
on the roof of my life
voices cry out
like the howling winter wind
the pain, the misery.

Prince of death take me
sweep me to your chest
lift these burdens of life
let my fond memories be flowers
smiles, honeysuckle, laughter
water lilies on the pond of my existence
and time like a glass of sand wind down
and let the axe rise over my neck and fall
evermore, evermore, evermore, as I fall
into the sun and become one with the universe.

In Case I Die Tonight

Is it possible to confess the great affection
yes, the love, the deep abiding love
the soul searing, teeth gnashing infatuation
two people can feel for one another?

Is it possible to admit the caring
the crying need, the longing
the desire and passion
two people can feel for one another?

Is it possible to tell the respect, the esteem
the mind and thought-sharing joy of
conversation over little things
as well as big?

Is it possible to convey
the deep empty feeling
the loneliness, the hunger, the depression,
two such people feel when they are apart?

Probably it is impossible, but in a simple way
without fanfare, let us share these thoughts
for a moment
for today
for eternity
and as they wash over us
like the sea over the sand
and we feel their harmony in our souls
let us hold hands and test their meaning
their truth.

The Professor's Creed

I am not the placid water
but am the turbulent sea
If you seek tranquility
do not seek me
What you stand for
I stand against
Discord is my virtue
Harmony is my bane
Doubt is my tool
Curiosity my ally
Acceptance is my enemy
Rejection my success
Darkness my light
Bigotry my frontier
Ignorance my wilderness
Rebellion my peace
Debate my composure
Conflict my messenger
Knowledge my goal
Yea, though I walk through the valley
of the shadow of conformity
I will never be like you
My reward is your condemnation
My motivation your grandchildren's acclaim

We All Do

Let me lay
on your altar
we all must
at one time
or another
the question is
what price our virtue
the root of evil
power
prestige
revenge?
Does it matter whore?

P.O.W.

Hungry eyes in shaved heads
Muscles trembling in the living dead
Blood-filled bugs in every bed
People killed for a crust of bread
Always hungry but rarely fed
Moving slowly as if filled with lead
Morning sun brings only dread

Toothless mouths from inadequate diet
Many who die without a fight
Buzzard circling like a big black kite
Desiring to eat of this human blight
Cruelty of guards with savage delight
Protected from victims by armed might
Love of country don't make it right

Kids Aren't Dummies

A car ran over a hop toad last night
Me and Butch were riding by on our bikes
It didn't make much of a noise
Just made a kind of squish
Probably, old Mrs. Johnson, who was driving
Didn't even notice
The toad was just sort of sitting there
On the paved road, eyes wide open
Mouth closed, waiting for a bug
But instead he got a tire, pow
Right across the old body
After, when the car was gone
We went back
His eyes were still open
But now they were big like nickels
And he was flat like a pancake
The tire made him larger
Bullet, my dog, who was also along
Growled at him and hit the toad
With one of his white paws
Then his paw was all red
'Cause the hop toad had leaked
It sure surprised me how easy
It was to touch that old toad
Usually it's real hard to touch one
Guess the car slowed him down
Mom says don't, cause they give you warts
I've tried, but they hop too fast
Butch has some warts
But he can't catch hop toads either
And says he never did
It's hard to know who to believe anymore
Mom also said that alcohol would stunt your growth
Just don't know, dad drinks and he's great big

Ode to Perfection

Here my love is a wish with cheer
May your days be numbered in the millions my dear
May you always have your smile so sweet
Your sparkling personality that makes you so neat
Your rosy lips and complexion so fair
Your penetrating eyes and soft beautiful hair
Your mind as free as an ocean breeze
Your life as clean as winter's first freeze
And here's a wish, the last of all
Don't make a change be it ever so small
For most people need a change like me
But then, they're not perfect as perfect as thee

I Am Weak

Eyes are so revealing
And that is why it's difficult
To look into yours, you might notice
My falling toward the brink

So if my face is turned
It's only a feeble attempt
To hide the honesty
For if I looked

My rough hands
Would draw you close
And caress your lovely body
Until buttons fell like rain

So, if I look away
Don't whisper my name
For I am weak
And cannot refuse your love.

You Might Say I'm Weak

Can a person be filled with another?

Can people be quenched
until time passes
and they become thirsty again?

Loneliness might creep in
finally causing a missing
a desire and need.

Personally
if this is the case
you might say I'm weak.

When we're apart
after leaving our love-warmed bed
your scent still lingers.

An overwhelming loneliness
possesses me
within seconds it becomes a dread.

A senseless, insecure dread
a dread of time
a dread you can't or won't return.

The next day is an eternity
memories are still fresh
distinct in my mind.

Our skin, our lips
your smile of happiness
so little and, yet, so very, very, much.

Yes, if love is like a tank
to be filled then emptied
you might say I'm weak.

Because
my tank is always empty
when we're apart.

Words Don't Matter

Wat you says don't matter
It's wat people thank you means
Consider him who says dat he likes you
If you cares for him dat means he luvs you
If you jus likes him den dat means he likes you
To dos whos any other case it mak's no deference
So jus lemme say I likes you
'Cause its wat you hears dat matters

A Drummer of Your Choice

And all were in black
And all stood and chanted
The tragedy, the despair
The misery for one so young
To take his own life.

And God called me before his tribune
And he asked, "What were you
in your worldly life?"
And I replied, "Mostly a failure."
And he asked, "On whose terms?"
And I answered, "By the standards of my peers."
And he said, "Of your fellow man?"
And I replied, "Yes."

He said, "Herein lies your major sin
the sin of the importance of your fellow man
Do you believe that man who knows love
who knows hate
who knows jealousy
who knows bigotry
Can ever see my face?
Can read my mind?
Can discern the indiscernible?"
And I replied,
"No, but it was necessary to die to find this out."
And he answered,
"Herein lies hell in which
you lived all your worldly life
and it consists in the main of living
under the direction of one's peers."

"Think of this," he said,
"Is God one or more than one?
Is God a free spirit or restrained?
In the end, do you face me alone?
Where are your friends and neighbors now?
Will they share any of your blame?
Will they burn one second for the sins
they helped you commit?
Oh, better that your pace had followed
a drummer of your choice
You would not be in the trouble you are now."

And I cried out in great
sadness and despair:
"Will I burn, Lord?"

And he answered, "No, my son, you have already paid
the penalty of your sins
Go now, to Heaven where all are God-like
And live as individuals as they would in the wilderness
Pure and free from the corrupting influence
of their fellow man."

While Reflecting on a Dream I Ran Into Regret

Dreams are often difficult to remember
but yesterday morning after arising
from a sleep-tossed bed
twisted and turned
like a wind-blown sea
a tear-streaked face
reflected from the mirror
the image taunted, it asked
can you recall this dream of sadness?
Tucked away in the subconscious
only allowed out a night
to quietly steal peaceful sleep?
This reflection spun wheels in reverse
backtracking through the halls of time
until they stopped at a door with a star.

Although you don't have to be a star
to play the lead in my hit parade
the door swung open and there you were
or there we were as the lights dimmed
the camera started, we danced across
the stage of life, a good relationship
even great by most standards
warm and nice, tender and beautiful
but a natural resource unexploited
reserves of happiness undeveloped
times of love, times of smiles,
denied days of laughter, nights of joy,
never shared until, too late.
Yes, dreams are often difficult to remember
but not the source of those particular tears.

Adversity

Adversity can lead to love
So come let us fight
Let us argue
Let suffering and pain surround us
The death of loved ones
Personal illness
Failure
Frustration
And from this tribulation
And through it
We will endure and live on
And the ugliness will
Temper our love into a strong bond
Unbreakable
Until death do us part.

What Might Have Been

We never know
what was not
nor could have been
but regrets
like a river flow
to speak of opportunities lost
swept away like twigs
before the rising burdens
which obscure
the past
the present
but sadly, foretell the future.

Why Love?

Loving is a sign of weakness
tenderness depletes strength
affection is degrading
sharing destroys individuality
saps the strength
brings the risk of hurt
the loss of peace of mind
so, why love?

Trouble

Thank you for the trouble
for the turmoil
without problems
with only smooth sailing
we tend to skate alone
never planning our route
taking the path of least resistance
never realizing we're lost.

Never

Success is the natural high of life
those who achieve it
become intoxicated with living
their confidence blossoms to love of self
and love of being
but unfortunately the way is narrow
only a few can tread the path
others must be satisfied with less
they mass below unable to reach such lofty heights
soberly facing life as an enemy
never drinking it in, never allowing it to go to their heads.

What power deems it so
some hidden strength
or weakness?
our parents dear?
God above?
Lady luck?
Birth and life
may be miracles
but what of living?
And what of achieving?
Must it always be so?

Why are there so many new churches
when people in the world
are starving to death?

Are churches built as a temple of God
or are they built to prove one community
loves God more than another?

When so few can achieve success in life
is it any wonder that many concentrate
on a life after death?

As economic well being improves
people think less of a life after
death and more of a life during life.

If during your present life you have the means
to fill your every want, would you be preoccupied
with an afterlife where your every want would be filled?

Looking

And looking into the valley
I saw birds on the wind
and ants
and trees
and other living things
striking was the beauty of nature
and tranquil was of silence
and I bespoke to myself
of lonely things
of oneness
of purpose
of the nature of being.

Clock of Time

Soldiers marching one, two, three
frogs chirping in a tree
people loving, like you and me
time passing will set us free
to this certainty we are not blind
it is a bondage of nature's kind
as God in Heaven will surely find
our clock of age a way to wind
and finally bring us to his breast
to join the host he loves best
ending our journey of eternal quest
to answer a question which seems a jest
but now we flit about the sky
never seeking the reason why
billions live and all must die
from the complex being to the tiny fly
were we still alive we might ask, why?

How I Grew to Love Daylight

Last night
in the early morning
I awoke with a fear so real
stark terror gripped my heart
it drove a fist into the pit of my stomach
my flesh was wet with sweat
I held my breath remembering the pain of the words:
"I don't love you"
"I don't miss you when you're away"
"I don't long for your touch nor want you close to me"
"We must part."

These words burned my ears
echoed through my brain
possessed my thoughts
and then, as before, they left me,
left me, to realize they were, but a dream,
a dream that lurked within,
a chained monster to be unleashed
from its nightly lair,
to devour,
to rent and tear,
all in the name of love.

Who Are You, Who Am I?

Who are you?
The person behind your eyes
In your mind
Will you tell me
Whisper it, scream it
Until the windows shatter
Your exterior is calm, placid.

But what hidden turmoil stirs inside?
Are the faults merely concealed
to make the outside compatible?
Is this you or the person people
want you to be?
Who are you?

Who am I?
Once naked and exposed
Now covered by artificial convention
Battered and buffeted along
Broken and beaten
Rejected and scorned
Until the reality is
Indiscernible from the fiction.

Am I free?
Am I me?

If You Will

Cast your dreams like broken bottles
on the highways of life.
They will shatter
exploding raindrops on a tin roof
glittering like tears
that will run down God's face
as he turns his back to shout
"This is no child of mine."

Who gave you reason?
Who gave you choice?
This you would throw away
and become a quitter?
Whose reflection is in your mirror?
Whose hand on your arm?
Whose brain in your head?
You are absolutely, uncontradictably unique

There is no like person
no like substance
life in any form
on earth or in the universe
comparable to you
and you would give up this birthright?
Best you live forever
no warm bed awaits you in the after life

The toll man waits
to exact his due
and you will not pass
without payment
to a ride of little joy
for an eternity
so cast your dreams away
if you will.

Blind

Unwanted like a kicked dog
crawling for love
for acceptance
to be put off by the cruelty
of rejection
the inhumanity
until we throw ourselves into traffic
like a blind armadillo
destined to be crushed
never a chance to learn from experience
just a smear on life's highway
everyone turns their nose up
afraid they will be tainted
by our tragedy.

Old Things

I love old things, old coins
old cars, old stamps, old bottles.

Perhaps, because they recall a more stable time
a time when people weren't in such a hurry
a time when simple pleasures were enough
a time when all problems were small problems.

So, I love things old
especially those good old days.

Yes – The Most Beautiful Word

And God spoke, saying:

I come with a sword not an olive branch
brother will be turned against brother
daughter against mother
and father against son.
In a way, a much simpler
but similar way
I say the same
forsaking all others.
Take my hand
walk with me along life's rough way.

Will you chance it while we can
before the ravages of time take us?
Will you give up those you love?
What of your parents and mine
Of your friends and mine
Can you be all to me
My Christmas
My Thanksgiving
My companion
and friend?

The Condemned Man Against the Wall

Tied hands
grasp the roughness
of the stone
taking comfort in pain
in knowing
only living flesh feels.

These rocks once tread
as a road
now stand
a wall
an end
or, still a road?

And as the guns rise
my mind shouts
what price freedom
so dearly bought
to lay me down
for political thought.

If You and I Were We

It is night again
You are gone
Loneliness returns
A well-known foe
But we will not share the dark tonight
Or sleep together
For memories sweep in
Leaves on the wind
Our first kiss
My stomach in knots
And the best day of all
When we sat and talked
When we dreamed of what could be
If only you and I were we

Early Fall

Automobiles tip-toeing over slick streets
traffic slowed down to a creep
people rising early from their nightly sleep
off to work in silence deep
broken only by cracking limbs
under nature's burden, a natural trim
children sliding all around
on icy blankets that cover the ground
a frozen pond that won't ripple till spring
along with the flowers it will bring
frogs and turtles sleep in the mud
cows in the barn chewing their cud
God in heaven watching it all
the job he created, early fall.

Original Sin

And of all things perfect
they made you in their image
whatever your parents are
you will, for a large part, be
they teach you to be loving
to be selfish, to be cruel
to be kind.

If you murder, they should be tried
if you sin, they should go to hell
you will never escape their teaching
their bigotry, their hate
and in a never-ending cycle
you will rear your children
with their values.

Me, Myself, and I

Come with me to a private place
where others cannot go
where light rarely reaches
where rivers never flow.

Where love, fear, and passion
are players on the stage
and monsters from the id
cause the latest rage.

Where we'll jump into the air
and turn inside out
to find at once it is ourselves
this poem is all about.

Ego

Ego inside
fearless driver
so restless
a hulking brute
no chains can bind you
neck bowed
against all you stand
even me

Spring is Fall Reincarnated

Leaves sweep from the trees
cascades of falling colors
forming blankets of brown and gold
heralding the birth of fall's child
he comes with his mother's dying throes
and moans his sorrow at her end
throughout the cold days and nights
he maintains icy watch
over her death bed
covering it with white sheets
and then when the son is weak
mother appears reincarnated
with flowery cheeks
and welcomes to breast her infant
to rest until he feels her weakening
and rushes anew to decry
the ever-changing season

Nothing Asked in Return

My possessions are before you
sort and pick
take the best or the worst
take them all or any part.

Without you, they are meaningless
cosmetic assets, quite inanimate
vacuum fixtures in a hollow world
reflections in a mirror of invisible images.

They have value because of what
they allow a person to do
and they are worthless to me
if I cannot use them for you.

Plain Geometry

Lines crossing in the air
students frowning and pulling their hair
at a load they can hardly bear
such miseries of life don't seem fair.

Pity the teacher without a friend
for the rules he cannot bend
offers the students knowledge to lend
and gives them equations that never end.

Through the window an open field
a temptation to which they cannot yield
if their minds they are to build
discipline and attention must be their shield.

Some go crazy as a bat
forgetting exactly where they're at
through the window as quick as a cat
just empty spaces where they once sat.

Teacher continues almost alone
never noticing most students are gone
working problems for one old crone
could teach the others, but only by phone.

Many have now climbed a tree
breaking the chains they are free
and in a place they would rather be
than face the bondage of geometry.

Basketball

As the home team
drives down to score
the crowd rises
blindly they chant "entertain us"
don't be disappointing
we are bored, we come here
to escape our lives
burdens of the world are lifted
from our shoulders
maybe we'll forget tomorrow

We reject simple pleasures
once you've seen one flower
you've seen them all
semi-naked bodies
are better than flowers
each one so different
most unlike peas in a pod
why are some tall and some are short
in any event, all flowers look alike
and even smell the same

Perhaps the game
will go into overtime
will you ever remarry?
No, because no one keeps
the vows anyway, I never did
Rat-tat-tat through the hoop
what a shot, very unlike any
of the other hundred made tonight
Perhaps we'll see another
aren't black bodies beautiful?

Oh, country clean, oh stream so clear
oh family love to fill with cheer
why did you desert us?
no one to visit us when we miss church
did you see that? the referee is blind
okay, okay, a foul, about time
now we get to see a foul shot
Did you know
there were 237,904 foul shots
in the NBA last year?

Who is your neighbor?
probably a freak
who knows, who cares
I slept with his wife
what's her name?
Barbara or Betty, I didn't ask
Say, maybe he'll shoot left handed this time
Oh mother, Oh father
the weight of it all
take me back into your dreams

Death

Death like a vapor
leaked into my thoughts
one day to linger
smoke on a rainy day
the grim reaper
hung about
to beckon
with moss-covered fingers
inviting the weary
those with little hope
or happiness
to step to the next plane

Gosh

Gosh, you're pretty
Gosh, you're sweet
But oh my gosh
you're mean

She

She asked me for a poem.
But none came to mind.
The more I thought, the less I saw.
Surely I'm going blind.

Soldier's Theme

Alone we fight in a lonely land
We pass the nights the best we can
We live to die and die to live
That right may vie and wrong forgive
We hear that we fight for our country dear
We wish we were there and she was here
For our interests few are easy to see
To hell with this and set us free

Clothes

If my life could buy a love
Gladly would I pay
To bring the sunlight from above
And many a happy day
For barren is the life of those
Who have the body
But not the clothes

Return

Often when life's burdens
become very heavy
my knees fold up to my chest
and I return to the world

Between unborn child and maturity
so provided for and comfortable
how enjoyable to be cared for
loved with nothing asked in return

But all too soon reality returns
to slap my behind and the world
with all its responsibilities
comes hauntingly back

It's Too Late

Weary eyes that watch the rat races
Workers who hate the treadmill they pace
Identify the decay of society it traces.

Lines of people who step in time
Bound by chains of a special kind
To fill spaces in an endless line.

The greedy rich who gather the wealth
Never stop to consider their health
Relish the role faith has dealt.

Their eyes are blinded
by the money they love
and cannot see the buzzards above.

My Only Crime

Love took my heart
Watermelon thief
And spit the seeds
On the ground
And everywhere one hit
Tears spread
Crystal flowers
That never bloom
Hollow body
Burden of mine
Falling for you
My only crime

While You Were Gone

Seconds
Hung about
Bats
They would not fly
Cancer patients
They would not pass
But lingered
Until you returned

Unfinished Spider Web

Spider web spun in the air
People walk by and it gets in their hair
Making it useless as a bug snare
Spider crawls hungry back to its lair
Life's so hard it does not seem fair

People with web on their head
Walking with feet full of lead
Signs all around, seen but never read
Strive all week to buy the daily bread
Life's so hard many wish they were dead

Baker at the counter, hands covered in white
Started to bake at dawn's early light
Will work all day and late into the night
To feed and clothe the family, a difficult fight
Life's so hard just doesn't seem right

The Trade

Standing on a watermelon
Just watching the ladybugs
Eating the tomatoes
A man on his way up
Or maybe just on his way
Thinking of brown-skinned
Ladies left behind
Their love traded for passion
A reality for an abstraction
Was the exchange fair?
Heaven only knows

Why Don't

Why don't the best nine little leaguers
get to play the most baseball?
Each team member plays an equal amount
whether good or bad.

Why isn't winning important anymore?
Why do we have pass-fail grades?
Why have summer camps stopped
having competitive events?

Competition makes aggressive people
Makes people want to rise above the crowd.
Be winners
Perhaps

There is no place for winners in the future
of the United States
Oh, Jolting Joe,
Where did all our heroes go?

The Right to Bear Arms

There are those who would take our lands
take these lands from our hands
take the freedom that we love
freedom to own guns to hunt the dove
but those of us who have freedom now
drove the horse that pulled the plow
cleared the land to till the soil
spent our lives in endless toil
and brought us to this lofty place
a wealthy nation, a super race.

Some say, "God created the land for all"
and wish a great nation would stagger and fall
but where were they in the August sun
when crops were to be harvested
and work was to be done
sure it's great to be an American today
but it hasn't always been that way
once people struggled just to survive
and their hard life made our nation thrive
tempered it for a Watergate.

When weaker people would've lost faith
now there are people who would rule in our place
and limit our freedom with a boot in the face
but before kicking me they'd better beware
you don't push a feather at a grizzly bear
I didn't get here being afraid of a fight
and strongly believe in one basic American right
the right to bear arms throughout our life
to preserve our freedom and prevent such strife.

Future Shock

Pushed by the past
pulled by the future
the present is knocked askew
it trembles, it shakes
no firm footing to be found
the people fall
their churches tumble
their capitals drown in rhetoric
their economies collapse
and all are drawn
into the vacuum
to emerge reborn again
tempered by failure
reformed by tribulation
to face the change
that occurs too fast
and birth, a society
eventually to last

Water Course, Of Course

Two streams meet in a swirl of water
Their bodies thrashing to become one
Twisting and turning, they dart to bed
Covered by friendly trees
Shaded by leaves and branches
They caress over mutual rocks
Until they consume each other
and accomplish what neither can alone
the birth of a river

Till It Quits Hurting

Locust hum a song
to loneliness
while listening
my mind asks
how long
must this be endured?

The thought
echoes back
to answer
forever
unless
you return.

I Want You to Know

I am sad
Extremely sad
For I have lost a love
Without ever having known it
Except within my soul.

I want to cry out against the decree
Of God and Man
That says we shouldn't be
To love only one person
Is asking a candle to burn forever.

But know although many candles may be lit
Only one can survive at a time
For the strongest
Will sap the oxygen from the air
Leaving little for the other flames.

Yet, despite the risk
I want to know all of you
Inside and out
and sit down and talk
With our feelings laid out.

But to do so may be to fall in to each other hopelessly
For my will is weakened and I lie on the brink
Of what? Of love? Of desire?
Of these I thought I had plenty
And had never wanted more.

So why now! What drives me?
Do I know you so well that I should risk
Blowing out one candle before the other is properly lit?
Why should I lead my heart away from familiar paths
And follow dreams that may not last?

Of me you know little
Except my responses
To your words of black on white
Words that make me see beautiful colors
And some that are mirrors of my mind.

Perhaps it is a paradox that so intrigues me
How do you know me so well when you don't?
You are unfair for you leave the decision to me
And yet you are just
For you know what may be.

My heart is torn in-two
By feelings of trust
From others who believe in me
And know me
And take me for what I am.

Yet each day you win another battle in my heart
And unless I join all my forces together
I will surrender myself to you
And I know I won't be harmed
Though others surely will.

The years between us are a bridge
To be crossed
I would rather live for today
Instead of tomorrow
And experience joy rather than sorrow.

Is it not better to love
Filling every day to the brim
Rather than let love pass by
But your years work against me
In yet another way

For they have made you cautious and wise
And it is your wisdom and farsightedness
That keeps me in rein
For I want to bite at the bit that restrains
And be free to run with you

But reality weighs my thoughts
As the rein is drawn tighter
And I wonder if I am strong enough to break away
I have much to learn from you
But how much, I may never know.

For from today I shall bind my actions with discipline
And discourage my thoughts of you
But if somehow I find a way to bond us together
Yet leave each of us free
I will use it for us and hope we will be...

The Man in the Buffalo Headdress

Around and around the fire he twirled
A rattlesnake rattle in one hand
Bone powder in the other
Magnified against the trees
His shadow larger than life
Flickered and danced in the leaves
Now here, now there
Of no real substance
As it was then, it is now
Large shadows are possible
But who can afford the bone powder?
And buffalo heads are so hot
And dancing near the heat isn't so neat
Perhaps this is why many prefer to cast a small shadow

Think of Me
(Ode to God)

When life's burdens press on your shoulders
weigh on your mind, furrow your brow
when the coffee spills on your new slacks
and you've had enough last straws
to break a hundred camel's backs
and no one will share the load
or buy you another cup for the road
think of me because when no one
else will, I will.

When you've fallen
into a snake-filled pit
and don't know what you want
but this ain't it
and the best of your friends
thinks you're a lout
and there is no one left
to bail you out
think of me, I will.

And if you live ten million years
and your ears always ring
with the crowd's cheers
and if we joke through all our tears
you'll never find a more certain fact
that day is light and night is black
that fish must swim in the sea
and that when you are troubled
you should turn to me because
when no one else does
I still do love you.

The King of Slapstick

He was the King of the Slapstick and
when he spoke, they listened:

"Is this a ploy, me boy
to gain or an end, me friend
or simply to annoy, my joy
do you pretend, to offend
as you enjoy, being coy
or do you intend, to befriend
as you employ a decoy
to mend and ascend?
If so, ahoy!
Let us join your convoy."

We Know You By Another Name

December 14, 1862

General Kershaw, CSA, was upstairs
From a window he surveyed a field
In front of a stone wall
It was covered in Federal blue
Mostly the bodies were still
Occasionally a small movement –
At least 5,000 were in sight
The result of the murderous battle of the previous day
Six times these brave Federals attacked
In wave after wave they fought
and died or were violently thrown back
Only darkness quenched their determination
Up the stairs came 19 year old
Sergeant Richard Kirkland, CSA
A son of South Carolina
Indignation was upon his face
"General I cannot abide
The suffering and pain of the Federals
All night and all day they've cried for relief
Can I go over the wall and give them water?"
The General turned with a look of dread
"Son, you wouldn't last 10 seconds
Before they shot you dead"
"Yes, sir, I know all about the risk."
Admiration filled the General's eyes
Such a noble young man,
"You may go and may God protect you."
General, may I use a white flag?
"No, if you go, you must go without one."
Kirkland said, "I'll take my chances."
Down the stairs he ran taking two at a time
He snatched up five or six canteens
Filled them with well water
Over the wall he went
Soon the Federals spotted him
Rifles roared
Bullets whined and sang

He made it to the first soldier
Leg broken beyond repair
Likely by a cannon ball
He cradled the man's head
And held the water to his lips
After he drank, Kirkland gently put the
Soldier's head on a knapsack
And continued across the sea of bodies
So thick he could not touch the ground
To the second gravely wounded man
Bullets still screamed but slowed then stopped
As his mission of mercy became obvious
He crossed the wall for more water
And back to the field again and again
Working in the reverent quiet for almost two hours
Until not a single Federal had want of water
Then this Ministering Sergeant returned
To his comrades behind the stonewall
As he disappeared, a few small hoorays
started on the Federal side
They spread across to the Confederates
Until a thunderous cheering and clapping
exploded from both sides
His fellow soldiers of Blue and Gray knew
His action was above and beyond the call of duty
Far more than ordinary courage was required
To risk his life to succor his enemy
For this Richard Kirkland was given no medal
Just a new name
The only one we remember today
"The Angel of Marye's Heights"

Lieutenant Richard Kirkland died less than a year later in the Battle of Chickamauga in September 1863. Believers will think he was reunited with his friends when he got to Heaven, although I doubt they know that many of them were wearing Blue. His dying statement was reported to be: "Save yourselves, tell Pa I died right." Indeed you did, Richard, indeed you did.

Nineteen years old and already a legend until the end thinking of others. Should we all die so grand?

Antietam: In Rows They Lay

The corn field changed hands thirteen times by noon
A rolling battle the crack of doom
The corn stalks were shot off at the ground
No cover for the weary anywhere around
Harvested like corn in rows they lay
The final result of the game they played

Rebs were in a sunken road
The field around was freshly hoed
Federals attacked this bloody lane
Around the sides they eventually came
Harvested like corn in rows they lay
The final result of the game they played

Today flowers watch over all
Brave men who answered the call
Never dreaming they would fall
The most killed in a single day
Harvested like corn in rows they lay
The final result of the game they played

Let Us Cross Over the River and Rest Under the Shade of the Trees

He stood as a wall
On the left flank
At "Bull Run"
The glory of the day
On him a mantle lay
His tombstone stands in testimony
Here lies Thomas "Stonewall" Jackson

A Battle Shaped Up

On Henry House Hill
The air was a humming
Death was a strumming
The Blue were a coming

Muskets clattered and men fell
The bullets pinged clear as a bell
Soldiers shook in mortal fear
Whispering of those so dear
And the Blue kept coming

Through a hail of lead
General Barnard Bee said
"Sure is hot under this attack
It will be much cooler if we step back"
And the Blue kept coming

Bee looked to see
A gray line held steadily
Beautiful as a spring in the dell
"Mountain Boys from Virginia," he yelled
And the Blue kept coming

That's Jackson standing like a stone wall
Seems to have no fear at all
Jackson turned with a nod of his head
Rally with us he bravely said
We will snatch victory today yet
Now, we'll give them the bayonet
With turkey gobbles and rebel yells
A river of steel descended the hill
And the Blue started running

Jackson's Bayonet Charge at the First Battle of Bull Run

Up lads up to the top
The blue will never stop
We've got the rebels on the run
Victory is in our grasp
Send this shoeless rabble south
We're at the crest
Just a few more steps
Them they'll surely run

What? I thought I heard a turkey gobble
Yipping and screaming
Howls and yells
Demons from hell
It chills my blood
What's that gleam
The shine of polished steel
I see the end of my life
Reflected in those bayonets

Mindless panic seizes my throat
I try to scream and cannot
Without thinking I turn
It is downhill
But I can't go fast enough
My god, the sound seems to be gaining
I must run faster
Cold fear grips my bowels
I'm afraid I'll soil myself
Mother, mother I need you
The Blue kept running

Gettysburg

The first day
The Federals arrived from the south
The Confederates from the north
Each seemed to be headed home
Jubal found Howard on Sementary Ridge
Pushing him across the valley to Cemetery Hill
Day one to the Rebels

The second day
Lee attacks the Federal north flank on Culp's Hill
He is repulsed
He also attacks the south flank
Between the peach orchard and the Boulder Field
The federals are driven back
Day two is a draw

The third day
At first light on a gray morning
Rebels attack Spangler Springs and Culp's Hill
The Valley of Plum Run is red with blood
Seven hours of battle by noon, then a lull
At 1:07 a two-hour artillery barrage begins
Then 12,000 Rebs under General Picket
Charge into a suicide of Union fire
The Federals win
The Union is preserved

Robert E. Lee's Offense at Gettysburg

Across the meadow they came
A mile or more
The grass was knee high
It tangled in their boots
Small white flowers with yellow centers
Were scattered around
The land sloped up to a crown
Aptly named Cemetery Hill

They were breathing hard
Their rifles and ammunition were heavy
Sweat showed on their faces
These were southern men
Battle hardened veterans
Racing into a hail of lead
For a leader they believed in
But who really lost this day?

Was it a failure of the soldiers?
No, it was a mistake of leadership
Robert E. Lee's most dangerous
When on defense
His army was on Union land
The Federals had to attack him
All he had to do was
choose a time and place

He ignored his strength and
attacked the Federals

Antietam Melody

The Texas Brigade was in the cornfield
The sixth time this day
The Federals were driving the Gray
Cannon balls howled overhead
Bullets whipped by like hail
Defeat threatened
A scythe of death cut men and stalks alike
Corn fell in golden cascades
Men in waterfalls of red
Standing over his wounded Captain

A Brigade sergeant started singing about an old gray mare
She was lost in the wilderness
And so it seemed were they
Other rebels joined in
The melody rose over the battle din
The Federals hearing this song paused
What manner of men are these who die singing?
The rebels charged
The Federal attack failed
Exhausted, both sides marched away

Horror

Sharpshooters sniped at the Rebs
When I shot, one fell in the water
Later when we crossed the river
Someone turned his body over
It was my brother, Richard

Succession

The star in your universe
The prince in your kingdom
The heir apparent
Until you and mom died
Leaving me a king without subjects

Age

Memories of passion
Once real
Now dreams
Cry for release
Cats fight
They won't be quiet

Source

Fig leaves in the garden
In supplication raised
Reaching for the rain
Reverent praise

Editor

Gentle hands
Upon my words
Her voice never heard

OTHER WRITINGS

The Stranger

After walking some distance, I came to a clearing in the forest, and in the clearing was a man, and the man seemed young and yet he seemed old. And in his hand, he held a round stone and know you this stone was of various hues, but of the main part blue, white, and green. Intently, he gazed at the sphere. Arriving near him, I asked: "Sir, this is the land of my liege, who are you and by what purpose have you so arrived?"

Lifting his face from the stone, he swept the forest. Finally, like a hawk on a rabbit, his eyes settled on me, a baleful stare, a gaze so intense it penetrated to the core: "WHAT say you my child? This land my father has given all, you would order me from?"

Immobilized by his assurance but speaking with more courage than I felt: "Sir, it is my job why must thou harass me?"

"Child of mine, you do not want to hear my name or purpose. People fear me and what I demand. They flee before me, so, just call me pop."

"Pop, you say, what manner of name is that my lord?"

"DON'T call anymore lord—it angers my father."

"FATHER?"

"YES, Father, have you seen any burning bushes around here with a deep, deep voice?"

"No, no burning bushes, now about your name."

"Well, Pop is really just my initials."

"Initials?"

"Oh, well if you must, just call me prince."

"Prince of what? Are you royalty?"

"Well, you might say a King of Kings."

"Oh, a King, not a prince?"

"Well, both a King and a prince."

"Sir, if you don't want me to know your name, just say so." At that moment, the round stone turned into a white dove and flew off. "Sir, that was very impressive, are you a wizard?"

"No, but I thought the dove might jog your memory. I guess I could have made the river part, would that have helped?"

"No, we have never had a prince who was a King who was a wizard, that I remember."

"Suddenly, the man stood up and although he was not tall, he seemed to tower over me."

"Little man, I tire of this game. If you do not leave me alone, Mother Nature will turn your butter rancid."

"Oh, I suppose you know her too?"

"As a matter of fact, yes—you might say she is on my team."

"Oh, you have a team? You're a coach?"

"Well, in a way, I do show people how to win."

"Do people really take to your coaching?"

"Well, if they don't, I make it awfully hot for them sooner or later."

The Boon

Intro
Around and around, the wooden spoon was turned,
stirring the contents of the cauldron,
until some remembered consistency was achieved,
as the stirring ceased and the liquid turmoil stopped,
the reflection of a weathered face appeared,
the lips were moving in an ancient chant:

Wizard
"Eye of the chicken and tongue of the lizard,
produce the master for this humble wizard,
legs of the spider and beetle wing,
secret words in this gold ring,
to this spot the Devil bring."

Intro
Suddenly a flash of light,
a puff of smoke,
the eyes of the stone goat waxed red,
its teeth flashed white, against the night,
and it spoke with a deep and throbbing voice.

Devil
Who invokes the calling of the ancients?
Who seeks the lord of the damned?
Speak, or be cast into the eternal flames.

Wizard
Bowing to the now living stone goat,
the wizard spoke,
it is I a humble wizard requesting a boon.

Devil
Oh yes, I recognize you now
as the local Baptist minister,
and well due is your reward
as you have lead many people

to hell for me.

Devil
But be quick, my work stacks up.
People in ever-increasing numbers
are becoming sinners,
my following is increasing geometrically.
Why it's lucky I have this everlasting flame
agreement with God, the price of oil being what it is today.
Do you know how much energy
is required to burn one sinner
forever? Oh well, never mind
all this shop talk is probably boring
what's the favor?

Wizard
Oh, Lord of Black, eye of night,
beacon of darkness,
your majesty of lowness.

Devil
Yes, yes, enough—get on with it.

Wizzard
It's really very simple,
I want contact to be made with beings
from another planet.

Devil
Heavens no, or that is, hell no,
you ask too much, you would
ruin our whole game.

Wizard
What game is that my Emperor of Sin?

Devil
You know the one I'm winning
between darkness and light, evil and
good, wrong and right.

Wizard

But why would it ruin the game Sire of Black Goatdom?

Devil

Because man believes he is the sole purpose of this struggle
between God and I—or the soul purpose—I get those mixed up.
If man finds he is not, it will destroy his little ant mentality.

Devil

Besides it would make it look
like we favored the Zeenons
or Triadds over the Earthlings.

Wizard

These Zeenons?

Devil

What Zeenons, I never spoke of Zeenons
or Triadds, it's forbidden
to tell earthlings of Zeenons or Triadds.

Wizard

But of course you did, how else would I know?

Devil

Maybe God told you or ESP. Don't blame it
on a humble little black goad—with a big mouth.

Wizard

No, No, I wouldn't do that
King of Lies, Great Prince of Deceit.

Wizard

However, let us suppose that life existed
on another world,
what would it be like?

Devil

Oh, I suppose it would be like the Zeenons
or the Triadds much more
advanced than earthlings—no fun at all.

Wizard
How so, master of treachery?

Devil
Why they have conquered the aging process,
and we can't do a thing with them,
they don't die, why that's cheating.
They aren't even Devil fearing—
they live forever—everlasting life is nothing
if you live forever—it's disgusting.

Wizard
Yes, yes I see the problem,
you want good wholesome, er, that is
evil sinful people around who die.

Devil
Of course, of course, if we let the earthlings meet these alleged
Zeenons or Triadds—the earthlings might want to live forever
(like eating of the tree of knowledge and becoming Godlike or
Devil-like—or you know).

Wizard
You mean these extraterrestrials
live forever and we earthlings die?
Why that's favoritism,
God would never allow that you must be lying.

Devil
Believe what you will gnat of nothingness
what you believe is insignificant
and the goat was gone in a puff of smoke.

Punishment of Love

Once upon a time, long ago when the world was young and its people were innocent and unknowing, be it known to you there were two lovers, one was green and the other was blue. Now, in their land, be it also known, there was a cultural (moral) law that stated, "Green people may not love or mix with the blue." All the citizens, both green and blue, knew of this law and carefully observed it and, neither did the colors mix. But be it known Shyrinia (who was green) fell in love with Extverto (who was blue).

Shyrinia had been raised in a proper way, by a good family, a family who observed all the laws—both moral and legal—so when Shyrinia realized her love for the blue, much was her guilt. She rung her hands and pulled her hair and nightly tossed and turned, but to no avail—both the guilt and the love remained (deep ran the teachings of her childhood—of the elders and wise ones).

Eventually, her parents found out about this illegal love and Shyrinia was secretly relieved, after all, she reasoned all those who break the law should be punished. She found satisfaction when people shouted and said, "you are immoral—you breaker of laws." She felt even better when she was struck—especially in the face (as this was the greatest insult to her), and she knew she deserved the greatest punishment for her actions.

As the love and the relationship continued, she felt even more guilty and would always manage to leave clues to their meetings, which would be certain to be discovered so she should get her just reward. Often, she should say to Extverto "meet me tonight where the river runs into the sea." But she would rarely go—even this was punishment—probably the biggest punishment of all because, you see, Shyrinia truly loved the blue and by not seeing him was punishment for herself for the guilt of their love.

Finally, with all the trouble and turmoil, she was able to justify giving up her love, and for a long while, the great pain of the parting was satisfying because it was the ultimate punishment. But as the seasons passed, her thoughts often turned back to her blue and she realized:

Love is scarce and hard to find
Love is pure and unblemished
Love transcends all morals, laws, and all guilt
and no punishment is required where there is love.

Blue without you.

A Fairy Tale – But Not Really

Many years ago when the world was young and the people were pure, there was a lonely prince in the land of Azog, who by chance while out riding saw a lovely young princess from the neighboring land of Goza. Now be it known throughout the land, this prince was struck, sorely struck, by the loveliness of this child (who was only half his age). He staggered like a shot deer to the round table and called all his learned advisors to council and said, "Tell me what can be done, for my heart is filled with love and my mind with thoughts of this angel!"

The advisors said, "But my lord, the people of Goza are so different. They wouldn't understand your love. Also what of the Queen you already have, what of her parents and yours?" There would surely be war, and the prince grieved and grieved. He grew thin and gray, his mind wandered, for he knew the great suffering his love for the Goza princess would cause.

Time passed and he became accustomed to the pain, but one day while hunting alone, he rode into a small clearing and there on a little hill sat the beautiful Goza princess—like a moth to the flame he drew near, and she smiled saying, "My lord, I never thought we would meet alone," and he replied "neither did I." She held out her hand and he knew, henceforth, he would love her as no other.

She said, "My lord, I have admired your deeds, respected your ability, and loved you from a distance. It matters not what the advisors say, it matters not that our people are different, that we are of different ages, and I care not of the queen. My only thoughts are how I feel when I look on your face, when I hear your voice, the peace I feel when we are together, the pleasure of your company—many people say you are cruel and mean, but I only know you as you are with me—kind and loving."

And, low and behold, the years fell away and mattered not, and loneliness disappeared like smoke in the wind and the drums of war mattered not. The Prince was filled with love, and his mind filled with verse as love songs sprang from his quill.

And they lived happily ever after.

The Hermit

The hermit living in the desert never feels the hurt of a broken heart, but also he never feels the joy of love. No person can give of himself without risk. The risk of great love is the great heartache when it ends. In most cases, pleasure must be balanced against potential pain—to consider the one without the other is unrealistic in an unstable world. Often, however, fools will rush in grasping the one never thinking of the other until too late. Then burned and crippled like the trees after a fire, they are slow to forget and a new relationship is difficult or almost impossible.

Hold Back the Night

Bang, Bang, Bang
Thump, Thump, Thump
Whack, Whack, Whack
Bang, Thump, Whack
There it was again
repeated over and over
a hammering
a pounding.

Moving carefully through the velvet darkness
drawn by the strange noises
they came
to stand and stare
and to question.

What are you doing there my man?
Why do you scurry to and fro?
Back and forth?
What motivates such a desperate struggle?

Without reply, the hurried figure continued to work
first to a sheltered corner
then to a nook
then under a box
then behind a door
into every crack
every crevice
every place sheltered and hidden
he reached
he grasped
he pulled out the dark
the black
and placing it on the ground he drove a stake into it
but before he could finish
it would begin slipping back
to its source
back to the shadows and recesses it would flow.

Finally, exhausted, he spun in a slow circle and
slipped with a sigh of fatigue and despair to the earth.
Out of the crowd limped an old man.
He prodded the now still figure with a crooked walking stick
and said,
Why are you in such a state of torment?
What are you trying to do here?

The figure on the ground stirred slightly
and its gloom filled voice echoed between the walls
and off the bricks.
Hold back the night.
Hold back the night.
I seek to hold back the night
to prolong this solitude
between periods of madness
but it slips from my fingers.
It escapes me.

The old man shifted from one foot to the other
he scratched his chin and said
but it is impossible to hold back the night
the night in its flight
its flight to escape the light.
Why do you attempt so hopeless a fight?

Without reply, the figure rose to its feet
and spread its arms in an arch with the fingers touching high
over the head.
Between the arms, lights flickered
a screen coming to life.
A rainbow of colors suddenly illuminating the surrounding area
then a vague image began to take shape between the arms
plainly it was a girl
a beautiful girl, who spoke, in a weak and spent voice:
I am the spirit of yesterday
of times old
of days past
of sweet memories
of simple times
but I cannot be tomorrow

darkness has vanquished my light.

Then her image disappeared to be replaced by a faceless blur
moving and throbbing it crossed the screen.
And a strong and forceful voice said:
I am the spirit of the present and of the future
of today and of tomorrow
of your dreams
of your fears
and I will conquer the dark and possess you.
You cannot escape the reality of my being
this is certain as certain as the sun will rise
to destroy the night.

The crowd stood, for a time, mesmerized
then slowly they began to scurry to and fro
and to pull the dark out until the air was filled
with the sound of their hammering.

War as a Facet of Foreign Policy

And hearing the noise of the bombs bursting in air and the shells exploding through the night, God looked down upon the earth where his glance fell on a small school with a playground and stairs leading down to a street.

And as the bombs burst around, a small white round object was seen rolling down the stairs and soon God was able to identify it—a baseball. Following it was a tiny figure, with a worn baseball glove and the clothes on his back were burning. Before he reached the ball, he fell in a heap of flames. Great tears of compassion crossed God's cheeks and his voice like thunder in the night filled the heavens. It boomed across the valleys, and bounced off the mountains: "No, No, not my children, the tragedy, the despair of it all, the heart rendering pain, angel of mercy spare me."

And lowering his forehead into his arms to shutout the sight he said, "Better that world political leaders live forever, because they have harmed those I love—the children. When they die—they are mine. Then none will say, I am liberal, or I am conservative, or I am democrat or I am republican, or I am capitalist or I am communist."

But all will say, "Spare us, save us God! We did not realize the harm caused by false pride, by mistaken beliefs, by using war to accomplish foreign policy."

And I will crush them all in my palm and cast them into the eternal flames.

Heart of Stone

The high priest stood before the altar and raised his arms toward the heavens. In rhythmic chants he repeated the prayers. Many times he raised the sacrificial knife to the sun and as it flashed, the massive crowd roared their approval but then became silent as he lowered it to his side. Then as if returning from the land of the dreams, his step quickened and he moved toward his victim. He plunged the knife into his chest and reaching in, pulled out the heart. A mighty roar rose from the people. The priest, however, exclaimed in anger, "It's already cold, cold. We are going to have to quit taking these damn volunteers. What's the story on this guy anyway?"

One of the guards said "Someone he loved lied to him."

The priest said, "I should have known. Look at that heart, it's already turned to stone."

Thoughts About God

If God is all knowing, he knows before children are born whether they will be saved or go to hell. And yet knowing this, he allows their birth to occur. Many theologians say this is to allow the children to grow to the age of reason, so they can decide to accept or reject Christ. However, in every case, God already knows when they reach this age what they will decide. Thus, God is not really allowing man freewill but is allowing the majority to be born to go to hell, and even if he is allowing man freewill, what is the point as he knows the exact outcome in advance.

At the same time, many Christians would agree that God loves all his children equally and yet he allows some to be predestined for heaven and others for hell. How then, can he love all equally? We are told that God made man in his image, that we have come up from the oceans and will return to it (being manufactured from the clay and sand, etc.) that life was breathed into us. How then are we and all nature stuck with such an unlikely and cumbersome method of reproduction. Considering how children love to play in mud wouldn't the method God used for creation work better for man?

Does God cry for sinners when they reject him—it couldn't be from shock as he knows before they're born what will happen? Has God fixed and faked the game of salvation—since he is aware of the outcome of every game in advance? The only conclusions are:

(1) God is not all knowing,
(2) God does not love all people equally,
(3) Man has not determined yet what God wants or expects of him,
(4) God does not exist.

The Quality of Life

And the man in his grief, in his disheartened spirit, in his depression walked to the entrance to the cave and shouted, "Oh great and wise sage of the cave, oh one of wisdom and thought, hear me now and answer. What is love and how does it affect and relate to my life?"

Deep from within the darkened tunnel, a voice spoke: "Love has to do with time and so does your life. Life is but a brief interval, smoke in the wind, to be seen and then gone, only the most famous are remembered for even a short time. Yet, love is the better part of this interval. It improves the quality of life."

November to May

It is true, and this we know, unspoken though it has been, that I must die before you—time and nature decrees it—so frankly and openly let me speak of this—as it stands between us. I am too old for you and beg you to go away from me—before it is too late—before the fever of our love again courses through your veins to reach the heart. Once it has reached the heart, it will possess your mind and you will come softly to me to whisper of love (as the willows weep their sorrow at your words). You might think, he has the strength to turn away—he will turn away. This is not true, will I who am weak from the ordeal of giving you up once turn deaf ears to your precious words now? Can flowers turn away from the Sun? Nor can I turn away if you wish to return.

Presently, I have the strength to exist—to live a life of little joy, an empty life because it does not include you, but a life of sanity and survival. The danger is I might perceive your slightest desire to come back and I might hurry along the trail of the past, in hopes of the slightest encouragement, in hopes of hearing the smallest word of love from you, and though you might not intend, this sweet barb, hurled so softly, could pierce my heart, destroying my will to survive. Or even worse, it might break the bonds of my selfish desires and I might take you as my wife, and then, when I die you would be abandoned to the life I was too weak to lead (alone without you).

Would I wish the misery of my present life on one I love so much—never, never—so, if I try to hold you, or if I try to kiss your lips, if I whisper of our precious love—turn away, turn away—though I live in deepest dread you might heed this warning and hate the honesty that made me give it.

On Love and Marriage

It is said marriages are breaking up because they suppress self, because people lose their identity, and because the ego is demeaned. If this is the cause of increasing divorce rates, then I'm afraid marriage as a viable institution is dead. Let me try to give reasons and mainly it has to do with thoughts about love, and I believe we can agree marriage is supposed to be based on love. In my opinion, the more a person can open his inner self to a loved one, the more love there can be—in other words, if I told my lover about the inner me, the exclusive me, the me reserved for me and for someone I love and trust. And in turn, she responded, and as we shared this private world, we realized the trust, the faith of two people risking rejection, ridicule, and great hurt in an effort to draw closer and closer, we would draw closer.

> Come with me to a private place
> where others cannot go
> where light rarely reaches
> and rivers never flow.

The more we open ourselves, the more known to each other we would become. But in this knowing would come responsibility—the responsibility of the trust and faith placed on our shoulders by the mutual love, and herein lies the trap. That is, in seeking such love, we do give up much of our self because sharing is the enemy of selfishness. We do lose some of our identity and this may punish our ego. Perhaps, this is caused by false pride. If it is, all I can say is pride is the enemy of love, and like the lion and the lamb, by its nature will destroy love. But sharing, trust and communication are the necessary ingredients of love and if these lead to loss of identity and self—then so be it—for life is lonely, empty, and incomplete for those who have pride and ego and lose love. For me, give me love, yes, no matter the risk, give me love.

Life is Like a Rose—Each Day a Petal Falls

This rose, perhaps, the most beautiful of flowers, is symbolic of beauty but is a mere token of something far more beautiful and important—us, our dream, our love. But unlike this rose whose beauty will fade with time, it is my desire, my hope, my prayer, that the beauty of our love will be undiminished for eternity. That this love will be an inspiration for all who love despite obstacles, that it give them hope (as it has us), that it give them courage to face what must be faced, and last, and most selfishly—may our love always be as beautiful today as you are to me—for if it is nothing can stand against it.

The Story of Two Birds

This is the story of two birds—Brown Bird and Blue Jay. Now long ago when the world was young and all things were simple and animals and birds could still talk, there was this little bird hopping through life, living from day-to-day, just eating worms, pecking around, scratching in the dirt and doing other natural things as she grew up. This bird was not unusual as birds go, not like the peacock, a rainbow of colors, but was just a plain brown bird with sparkling eyes. Mostly people and those of the forest never noticed this bird because she was very quiet—never sang and blended into the brush so well.

But then one day, Blue Jay flew down, saying "Little Brown Bird, why are you so quiet—I know you can sing, and your beautiful voice could bring much joy to the world. Why do you hide it inside?"

Brown Bird was troubled, as she had always been quiet. Could she now sing? Finally, she answered, "Blue Jay, I've never sung and I fear the world might laugh at my songs."

And Blue Jay said, "Brown Bird, would you sing for me? You know, kind of like practice and I promise not to laugh at you."

Brown Bird trembled and shook, but Blue Jay placed his wing on hers and waited very patiently. Eventually Brown Bird said, "Okay, but just for you—and don't look at me as it makes me nervous."

Blue Jay nodded and turned his back—at first there were a few notes, then more and more and finally a torrent of penned up songs filled the forest. Suddenly, Brown Bird stopped and silence filled the woods. Blue Jay said, "Oh Brown Bird, why do you stop?"

Brown Bird said, "I am fearful and know those who keep songs inside need nor fear the hurt of the world."

Blue Jay replied, "This is true, but it is also true that they never share themselves because they exist on the world never giving, never opening up, never revealing their inner self."

Brown Bird thought for a moment and said, "Blue Jay, I've never had a friend. Would you be my friend? Would you teach me to sing, to share my song?"

Great tears came to Blue Jay's eyes and he said, "Gladly, would I do this Brown Bird, for I am also lonely and friendless, but God in Heaven gave me a raspy voice, a voice of little beauty—I'll be your friend and do anything for you, but it would be impossible for me to teach you to sing for you must do this yourself!"

Brown Bird was silent for a time, and then said, "But Blue Jay, it's not always the singing but often the words that are beautiful—would you try for me as I did for you?"

Blue Jay said, "Yes, but only if you'll hold my wing and look into my eyes and sing with me for although my voice is brave, my heart is weak and I need the strength your friendship gives me."

She took his wing and together they started to sing, first a few notes, then a torrent and soon the forest was filled with their song. Animals and people of the forest paused to listen, and as Blue Jay and Brown Bird opened themselves to the world, many were amazed at the beauty of their song. And in the years that followed, Brown Bird and Blue Jay sang and sang and opened themselves to the world. And the world was a better place because of them. Will you open yourself to the world? Inside of you is a natural beauty. Will you keep it from those who have need: the lonely, the unloved, from the one who loves you?